SEP - 9 2016

Spotlight on Colorado

THE PIKES PEAK GOLD RUSH

Peter Vescia

PowerKiDS press™

NEW YORK

Published in 2016 by The Rosen Publishing Group, Inc.
29 East 21st Street, New York, NY 10010

Editor: Debbie Nevins
Book Design: Iron Cupcake Design

Cataloging-in-Publication Data

Vescia, Peter.
The Pikes Peak gold rush / by Peter Vescia.
p. cm. — (Spotlight on Colorado)
Includes index.
ISBN 978-1-4994-1456-1 (pbk.)
ISBN 978-1-4994-1458-5 (6-pack)
ISBN 978-1-4994-1460-8 (library binding)
1. Pikes Peak Region (Colo.) — Gold discoveries. 2. Gold mines and mining — Colorado — Pikes Peak Region — History — 19th century. 3. Pikes Peak Region (Colo.) — Juvenile literature. 4. Colorado — History — Juvenile literature. I. Title.
F782.P63 V47 2016
978.8'56—d23

Photo Credits: det 4a09164/Library of Congress, cover; optimarc/Shutterstock.com, 3; Craig Mills/Shutterstock.com, 5; Heritage Auctions/File:1794 1C 'Venus Marina' (S-32) (obv).jpg/Wikimedia Commons, 6; CRIS BOURONCLE/AFP/Getty Images, 7; Baloncici/Shutterstock.com, 8; maplab/File:Map of gold production.svg/Wikimedia Commons, 9; Everett Historical/Shutterstock.com, 11; Utah State Historical Society Classified Photo Collection, Identifier 39222001341648/File:Samuel Brannan.jpg/Wikimedia Commons, 11; optimarc/Shutterstock.com, 13; Everett Historical/Shutterstock.com, 15; Everett Collection/Shutterstock.com, 17; Victorian Traditions/Shutterstock.com, 18; Gilles Paire/Shutterstock.com, 20; Jeffrey B. Banke/Shutterstock.com, 21; Hein Nouwens/Shutterstock.com, 21; Gilles Paire/Shutterstock.com, 22; Everett Historical/Shutterstock.com, 23; LC-DIG-pga-00517/Library of Congress, 25; Robert N. Dennis collection of stereoscopic views/File:The little kiddy's, Central City, Col., U.S.A, by Kilburn, B. W. (Benjamin West), 1827-1909.png/Wikimedia Commons, 26; Everett Historical/Shutterstock.com, 29; Perspectives - Jeff Smith/Shutterstock.com, 30; Nikki Montoya Taylor/Shutterstock.com, 31; Photomika-com/Shutterstock.com, 32; Corn/Shutterstock.com, 33; cph 3a19584/Library of Congress, 34; John C. H. Grabill/File:Grabill - The Cow Boy-edit.jpg/Wikimedia Commons, 35; Jackson, William Henry, 1843-1942, photographer/File:Denver Colorado 1898 LOC 09570u.jpg/Wikimedia Commons, 37; Denim Pete/Shutterstock.com, 38; Janis Maleckis/Shutterstock.com, 39; AP Photo/The Denver Post, Glenn Asakawa, 41; T Cassidy/Shutterstock.com, 41; Rcsprinter123/File:1860 colorado territory map.png/Wikimedia Commons, 42; Bobkeenan Photography/Shutterstock.com, 45.

Manufactured in the United States of America

CPSIA Compliance Information: Batch #BS16PK: For further information contact Rosen Publishing, New York, New York at 1-800-237-9932

Contents

CHAPTER 1

Yellow Metal

Two hundred years ago, Colorado simply did not exist. Oh, the land was here, of course—the vast, open plains, the mountains, the mesa country, and the mighty rivers. But the map of invisible boundary lines that made a rectangular-shaped section of this land into a place called Colorado—that did not yet exist.

People lived here, in the land that would become Colorado. Various tribes of native peoples inhabited these regions, as they had for centuries. Europeans—mainly Spanish—had occasionally passed through these parts. They came exploring and searching, but didn't stay. They never found what they came looking for. Gold!

The funny thing is that gold *was* here, and it still is. The earliest explorers expected to find fantasy cities glittering with gold.

IT'S GOT TO BE HERE SOMEWHERE!

In 1835, a fur trapper named Eustace Carriere got lost in the Rockies for many weeks. During his wanderings, he collected specimens that were later found to be pure gold. He led an expedition back into the mountains to get more gold, but was unable to find the same place again.

Unlike the earlier Spanish explorers, Pike's expedition wasn't a gold-seeking mission. His group was sent to discover and chart the newly purchased western territory of the young United States.

PIKES PEAK

The real gold, however, was hidden in the ground. The native people occasionally discovered sparkling bits in stream beds. But they had no use for the yellow **metal**.

Yet explorers and other newcomers continued to hear tales of gold. When Zebulon Pike led a U.S. Army expedition to the Colorado region in 1807, he heard the rumors, too. Pike never found any gold, either. However, just a few decades later, this great wilderness would become a booming destination. Pike would have been amazed!

IS THAT A MOUNTAIN I SEE?

Zebulon Pike never found gold, but he did find a mountain. Pikes Peak is named for the explorer, who was the first nonnative person to see it.

After declaring independence in 1776, the young United States had very little gold and silver (the great gold and silver discoveries would come later). It had plenty of copper, however, so the earliest U.S. coins were all made of copper, such as this coin from 1794.

CHAPTER 2

What's So Great About Gold?

Why is gold such a big deal, anyway? The native people living in the Colorado territory had no use for it. After all, gold is not food. It isn't clothing, shelter, weaponry, or medicine. Unlike tribes in Mexico and South America, the Indians of the American Southwest did not know **metallurgy** or metalworking.

Gold has no **intrinsic value**. That means it has no importance or worth in and of itself. Rather, gold has value because certain people *say* it does. And people long ago decided that gold is the most valuable metal in the world.

Throughout history, certain cultures used gold to bestow importance on other things. Royalty wore gold jewelry to signify wealth and power. King Tutankhamun of ancient Egypt, for example, was buried in a sarcophagus made of solid gold. In churches and temples, gold decorations convey a sense

The Inca Empire, the largest Native American civilization in the Americas, was on the west coast of South America. The Incas practiced mining and metalworking and were excellent goldsmiths. When the Spanish conquered the Incas in the 1500s, they captured many exquisite gold artifacts. Alas, they melted down most of artwork for its gold.

King Tutankhamun—often called King Tut—was mummified in a solid gold coffin, or sarcophagus, in 1323 B.C.

of divine majesty. We still use gold for this same purpose today.

People have also used gold to obtain other things. In other words, gold was, and is, money. Some cultures made coins of gold. We don't carry gold coins around today, however. They would be worth *way* more than a dime or a quarter—or even a dollar!

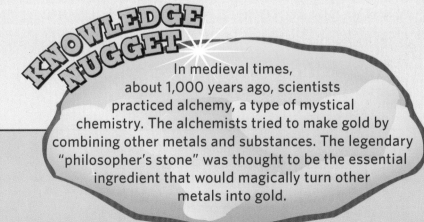

KNOWLEDGE NUGGET

In medieval times, about 1,000 years ago, scientists practiced alchemy, a type of mystical chemistry. The alchemists tried to make gold by combining other metals and substances. The legendary "philosopher's stone" was thought to be the essential ingredient that would magically turn other metals into gold.

Since ancient times, people have treasured gold for its beauty. No other metal occurs in nature in the same color. Unlike other metals, gold does not tarnish, rust, or corrode. It never loses its brilliance, even after thousands of years. No other metal is like gold.

GOLD BULLION

Although everyday coins are no longer made of gold, many governments, banks, and even some very rich people own gold **bullion**, or bars, as units of wealth.

Gold is also highly valued because it's rather scarce and hard to get at. If gold was lying around in everyone's backyard, it would be worth about as much as any plain old rock.

Most gold produced today goes into making jewelry. But in recent years, new uses for gold have been discovered. The metal's unique chemical and physical properties make it

*This map shows the world's gold production in kilograms. The
darkest-colored countries produce the most gold.*

200,000+
100,000 - 200,000
50,000 - 100,000
20,000 - 50,000
10,000 - 20,000
<10,000

useful in high-tech equipment. Gold performs
critical functions in computers, communications
equipment, spacecraft, jet aircraft engines, and
many other products.

Gold is mined in several places on Earth.
The United States is the world's third-largest
producer of gold, with China being the
first. Historically, three-quarters of U.S. gold
has come from just five states—California,
Nevada, Alaska, South Dakota, and, of course,
Colorado.

The total amount of gold in the world
(above ground) is thought to be about 188,826
tons (171,300 metric tons). That much would fit into a
cube measuring about 67 feet (20 meters) on all sides.

San
Francisco
grew from a
small settlement
of about
200 residents
in 1846
to a crowded
city of about
36,000 by
1852.

CHAPTER 3

The California Gold Rush

"Gold! Gold! Gold from the American River!" shouted Samuel Brannan. In May 1848, he walked the streets of San Francisco holding up a vial of gold dust for all to see. Brannan was a shopkeeper in Sutter's Creek. He had already begun stocking pickaxes, shovels, pans, and other supplies for gold **prospectors**.

A few months earlier, James W. Marshall had been building a lumber mill on the American River near Brannan's town when he found some gold flakes. The word spread. Even without phones, radios, or Internet, the news flew around the world to the far reaches of China, South America, and Europe, as well as to the United States' East Coast. The discovery soon set off the famous California **gold rush** of 1949.

People hoping to "**strike it rich**" soon "rushed" to California. Some 300,000 of them headed west to "**stake a claim**." But there was

Most of the Forty-Niners did not strike it rich. And many of them did not stay in California. On their way back East, some stopped in the Colorado territory.

Prospectors pan for gold in California in 1849.

no easy way to get there. The territory was not yet a state. In fact, it had only just become an official part of the United States after a war with Mexico. The gold seekers came to be called "Forty-Niners" in reference to the year. About half came by boat, and half came by land. Some of them passed through Colorado on their way.

KNOWLEDGE NUGGET

The gold rush changed California so quickly that it applied for statehood in 1850. It became a state that same year. As first, the state was unconnected to any other U.S. state because all the lands it bordered were territories.

Sam Brannan became "California's first millionaire." He owned the only store between San Francisco and the gold fields and began by selling supplies at greatly jacked up prices. He eventually bought up gold mines and vast amounts of land in California and Hawaii. Sadly, he died in 1889, broke and forgotten.

Confluence Park
in Denver marks the
location where Green Russell
discovered gold in 1858.

CHAPTER 4

Green Finds Gold

William Greeneberry Russell (1818–1877) knew a little something about gold. His father was a miner in Georgia during the Georgia gold rush of 1828. In 1949, "Green" Russell (as William was called) went to California along with the other Forty-Niners. Unlike most others, he did find gold. Not enough to get superrich, but enough to keep him interested.

Russell made several trips to and from the West Coast, **panning for gold** along the way in each direction. In 1858, on returning from California, he heard from some Cherokees about gold in the Pikes Peak region. Russell had married a Cherokee woman, so he had an in with the tribe. He and a small party met up with some tribe members who led them to the place where the South Platte River meets Cherry Creek.

Green Russell would hardly recognize his old prospecting site today—Confluence Park is a district of brick warehouses, rail yards, highways, concrete walks, and parking lots.

Gold prospectors used tools like these—a pickaxe, a wash pan, and a compass.

After nearly three weeks of trying, Russell and his friend Sam Bates finally found what they were looking for. In Little Dry Creek, a short tributary of the South Platte, the prospectors found about 600 grams of gold. It was the first significant discovery of gold in the Rocky Mountains. Russell went on to find more. And, of course, word spread!

THE GEORGIA GOLD CONNECTION

Dahlonega, Georgia, was the site of the largest gold rush east of the Mississippi River. Like Green Russell, many Georgia miners went on to California and then to Colorado in search of gold. Golden, Colorado, is named for Thomas L. Golden, an aptly named miner from Georgia.

CHAPTER 5

The Fifty-Niners

The discovery of gold in Colorado in 1858 set off a frenzy. It was not unlike the California gold rush of 10 years earlier. Then, the rushing prospectors were called the Forty-Niners. This time, the droves of gold seekers were called the Fifty-Niners, because the year was 1859. Quite a few of the Fifty-Niners had been to California in the previous rush. But many of the Colorado bound were simply hopeful first-timers.

They arrived in a wilderness that had little of the civilization they were used to—no hotels, restaurants, or stores. There were barely any roads, but that would quickly change!

The Colorado gold rush brought the first substantial influx of European Americans to the region. About 50,000 to 100,000 gold seekers came from all over. There were men, women, and children; whites, blacks, and Native Americans; doctors, lawyers, and politicians;

Some people, determined to beat the masses, set out for the Rockies in the final months of 1858. Once they arrived, however, they realized they wouldn't be able to start mining until the snow and ice melted. Those early birds had to tough out the Colorado winter while they waited.

In this early photograph, miners examine gold in a pan.

poor farmers, woodsmen, and former soldiers—and even some criminals on the run from the law. Almost all the prospectors were men.

What the Fifty-Niners had in common was a dream. They were fortune hunters. They wanted to "get rich quick." They wanted to "**hit pay dirt**." In short, they wanted better lives. This golden dream had sometimes been called the California Dream. Now it was becoming the American Dream.

CHAPTER 6

Pikes Peak or Bust!

The Fifty-Niners didn't think of themselves as traveling to Colorado. After all, the state of Colorado didn't yet exist. They would tell you they were on their way to "Pikes Peak Country." From 1854 to 1861, most of the eastern, plains portion of Colorado was officially part of the Kansas Territory.

Even though they were not headed to Pikes Peak itself, the gold rushers were called "Pikes Peakers." The people were actually heading to a region about 85 miles (137 km) north of Pikes Peak—to the place where Green Russell had found his gold.

Nevertheless, the motto for the hordes of hopeful became "Pikes Peak or Bust!" Many people painted the slogan on the side of their covered wagon, which was pulled by oxen or horses. Those were the lucky travelers. Other Fifty-Niners pushed wheelbarrows or carts. Some piled their provisions on a mule

Many gold rushers journeyed in covered wagons such as these. Long lines of wagons often traveled together.

and walked alongside. Others simply walked, carrying what they could.

Pikes Peak became the focus of the gold rush because it was the best-known landmark in that part of the country. Also, after trudging westward across hundreds of miles of grassy plains, the travelers would finally spy Pikes Peak on the horizon. Seeing the mountain was a happy occasion because it meant they were nearing their destination.

For safety's sake, many Fifty-Niners traveled in wagon trains. These were groups of covered wagons that journeyed and camped together. Some had milk cows tied to the wagons, to supply fresh milk along the way.

GOING WEST

There were no highways across the plains. By this time, however, there were several well-worn trails to the West Coast. But those trails went north or south of Colorado's Rocky Mountains. The Fifty-Niners quickly forged a more direct path, the "Smoky Hill Trail," west through the Kansas Territory. This trail existed from about 1855 to 1870. It ran for 592 miles (953 km) from Atchison, Kansas, to Denver.

No matter which route they took, most prospectors left civilization behind at the Missouri River. Hordes of people passed through St. Louis, Missouri. Many other towns along the river had their own crush of traffic. The towns took on a carnival-like atmosphere as the locals tried selling every imaginable thing to the people passing through.

The last significant settlement along the way was Manhattan, Kansas. After that, the travelers were pretty much on their own for the next 500 miles. The trip took about three to five weeks on average. Some groups got lost; some ran out of food or water. Some were attacked by Plains Indians. No one knows how many people died along the way to the Rockies. Very simply, nobody kept track. Nobody could.

The Joys of Modern Living
Today, the travel time from Manhattan, Kansas (now a city), to Denver, along I-70W, is about 6 hours and 48 minutes.

SEEING THE ELEPHANT

"I have seen the elephant" was a popular phrase during the 1800s. It meant you had experienced all the bad luck and hardship that life could throw at you. Discouraged gold rushers heading home often posted signs on their wagons—sometimes right over the "Pikes Peak or Bust!" sign—gloomily announcing, "I have seen the elephant!"

Panning rarely produces great wealth by itself. However, it can be a good way to locate the source, the gold **veins** in nearby rock formations, often underground.

CHAPTER 7

Panning for Gold

How do you search for gold? Do you just walk around, looking on the ground, hoping you'll see a shiny **nugget**? People *have* found gold that way, but it's not usual. Most of the early prospectors got started by panning for gold.

The process is simple. People still do it today, mostly for recreation or as a hobby.

Here's what you need: a shallow pan (it looks something like a pie pan); a screen or strainer to fit the pan (sort of like a sandbox toy); a good shovel; and a container for your specimens. You can bet the prospectors also had some strong, waterproof boots.

A gold digger pans in a river in 2014.

EVERY PANNER'S DREAM—A LARGE NUGGET!

Next you need a stream. It's best to find a stream where gold has been found before. The early prospectors couldn't all work the same stream, though, so they would try to find their own secret spots. But why a stream? Over time, in places where gold exists in the bedrock, erosion works bits of the metal out of the rock. Rain washes the grit into the nearest stream, and the rushing water carries the gold particles. But gold is heavy. In places where the water slows, the particles will sink into the **streambed**.

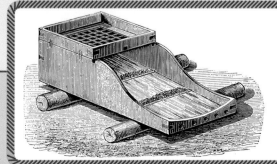

Prospectors sometimes used rocker boxes instead of pans. A rocker box can sift a larger amount of sediment than a pan alone.

Another shiny mineral that can trick inexperienced prospectors is mica. Crystals of mica are often found in rocks. It's pretty, but it's not gold.

Choose a spot in the stream where the water is about six inches deep. The stream should have a gentle current, not rushing water.

Fill your pan about three-quarters full with dirt from the streambed. Then hold the pan just under the surface of the water. Shake the pan vigorously back and forth and side to side. Twirl the gravel in a circular motion. Swirling the pan just under the surface of the water washes away the lighter sand and gravel. You will be left with heavy black sand and, if you're lucky, gold.

There are several methods for separating the gold from the black sand. One involves using a magnet. The black material is mostly made of magnetite, an iron mineral that is magnetic. Gold is not magnetic. If you have

found some gold, it will be in tiny nuggets and flakes. You can pick them out with tweezers. Place your gold bits in a small bottle or vial.

Since gold is about 19 times heavier than water, the bigger gold chunks stay close to the source, while the finer gold flakes and dust wash much farther downstream.

A gold rush prospector uses a sluice box to process larger amounts of sand at a time.

This kind of gold is called **placer gold**. This gold has been eroded from its source by natural forces, such as flowing water, and deposited elsewhere. Most gold rush prospectors found placer gold. The path to real wealth, however, was deep underground.

FOOLS BEWARE!

As William Shakespeare said, "All that glisters [sparkles] is not gold."

Novice gold seekers often confuse iron pyrite for gold. Many of the early prospectors found shiny bits of yellowish iron pyrite and thought they had hit the jackpot. That's why the common mineral is called "fool's gold."

CHAPTER 8

Angel of the Rockies

Aunt Clara Brown

Among the many thousands of people flocking to Colorado in 1859 was Clara Brown (1803–1885). She was not the ordinary gold seeker. In fact, she wasn't seeking gold at all, but rather her long-lost daughter.

Brown was born into slavery in Virginia. At the time of the Pikes Peak gold rush, slavery was still legal in the United States. Brown grew up, got married, and had four children—all of them slaves. When her "owner" died in 1835, Brown, her husband, and her children were all sold off to different slave owners. Her youngest child, Eliza Jane, was just 10 years old when the family was ripped apart. Clara Brown never knew where her family members were taken.

When she was 56, Brown received her freedom. Now where was she to go? She had no home, no family, no money. She set out

Clara Brown is thought to be the first African American woman to take part in the Colorado gold rush. She was Denver's first black female resident.

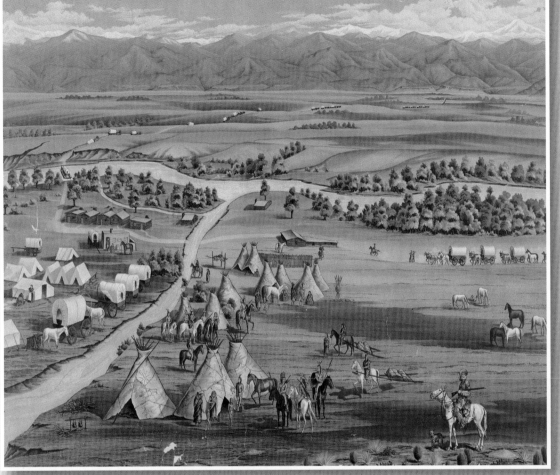

Denver looked like this when Clara Brown arrived in June 1859.

to find her youngest daughter. At the time, it seemed the whole country was suddenly flocking to Colorado. Brown got a job as a cook to 26 men heading for Pikes Peak Country in a wagon train. She walked most of the 700-mile journey to Denver.

This is what Mountain City looked like when Aunt Clara Brown lived there.

There, she set up a laundry business for the gold miners. She had plenty of customers! And sometimes there was gold dust in their pockets, which she collected. After a while, Brown moved to Mountain City (which later became

Central City) and set up her business there. A rich **lode** of gold, the "Gregory Lode," had just been discovered in a **gulch** in that area.

Brown operated her business and invested her earnings in real estate. She made a small fortune and became a rich woman. But she didn't live like one. Instead, Brown used her money to try to find her daughter. She also used it to help other people. She provided food, shelter, and nursing care to the townspeople and became lovingly known as "Aunt Clara." Far and wide, she was called the "Angel of the Rockies."

Toward the end of her life, Brown finally located Eliza Jane in Iowa. She brought her 56-year-old daughter to Denver to live with her, but Clara died the following year at age 80. She never found any of her other children.

Aunt Clara Brown was a strong, courageous woman who turned her sad life into a model of love and hope. She is one of Colorado's heroes.

A NOBLE WOMAN

At Clara Brown's funeral, Denver Mayor John L. Routt praised Aunt Clara as "the kind, old friend whose heart always responded to the cry of distress, and who, rising from the humble position of slave to the angelic type of noble woman, won our sympathy and commanded our respect."

KNOWLEDGE NUGGET

Hall of Famer
Clara Brown is considered one of the 100 most influential women in the history of Colorado. She was inducted into the Colorado Women's Hall of Fame in 1989.

CHAPTER 9

Mining Camps

Panning for gold was well and good. But the droves of fortune hunters quickly cleaned out what placer gold could be found in streambeds. Getting at the serious stuff required mining.

In May 1859, John Gregory discovered a gold-bearing **vein** in a ravine about 40 miles (64 km) west of Denver. As the news spread, other prospectors quickly found other veins nearby. The region around today's Black Hawk and Central City was called the "Richest Square Mile on Earth." Hard-rock, or underground, mining requires big equipment and a great deal of manpower. An individual cannot do it himself. Therefore, mining camps sprung up at Gregory's Gulch and at other locations throughout the Rockies.

Life in a mining camp was no picnic. Young men were often homesick and lonely—and

TIME FOR STATEHOOD?

In October 1859, a group of gold rushers attempted to create a regional government separate from the Kansas Territory. They established the new Jefferson Territory and immediately applied to the U.S. government for statehood. It was denied, and in fact, the Jefferson Territory was never officially approved. Nevertheless, the democratically elected government of Jefferson Territory managed the region for about 16 months.

UNDERGROUND MINING

those were the lucky ones. Living conditions were unsanitary and illness was common. The camps were built so quickly that there were few provisions for hygiene, never mind comfort. Streams were often used as toilets and garbage dumps. Food and clean water were a constant challenge. High-altitude living, for those not accustomed to it, made physical labor much more difficult. On top of all that, the weather in the high Rocky Mountains is cold, windy, and unpredictable.

If statehood had been granted to Jefferson Territory in 1859, today's Colorado (plus some of surrounding states) would likely be named the state of Jefferson.

29

Most miners did not get rich. What money they made went toward housing, food, drink, and living supplies in the new mining town stores.

Old mining camp buildings in the town of Ashcroft, near Aspen

Mining itself was hard and dangerous work. Miners inhaled rock dust from drilling. Some miners were injured, or even killed, in explosions or other accidents. There were no safety regulations in place. In fact, there was no real government at all, so mining camps often formed their own rules.

Although there were some women in some of the camps, most inhabitants were men. In the wilderness, many men stopped shaving and washing. Bathing and do laundry were very infrequent luxuries. Filth was everywhere. Food scraps and animal carcasses were often left to rot in place. As you can imagine, mining camps—and the miners themselves—probably stunk to high heaven.

Prices were extremely high in mining towns. It was very difficult for shopkeepers to get supplies to the remote, new mountain towns. Also, with so few stores, miners could not shop around for the best prices. There was no competition.

To combat the dreary living conditions, folks created their own entertainment. Men played music on real or makeshift instruments, and there was singing and dancing.

Just as quickly as mining camps were settled, they disappeared. If a mine was not producing enough gold to satisfy the boss, or if more gold was discovered elsewhere, the entire operation moved away. Those camps that stayed in one place, however, soon turned into small towns. The miners had money to spend, and it didn't take long for shops, saloons, hotels, dance halls—and even churches—to crop up to serve them.

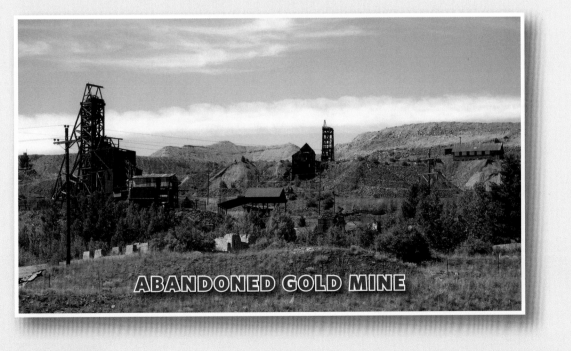
ABANDONED GOLD MINE

CHAPTER 10

Life in the Wild West

Within a few months, a mass of humanity arrived in the Rocky Mountain wilderness. Camps sprang up so quickly, there was little time to organize government or law enforcement. In many camps, miners elected a presiding official, a claims recorder, and sometimes a judge and a sheriff to keep order.

Shops, saloons, and gambling dens popped up almost overnight. Blacksmiths, carpenters, and other tradespeople set up businesses.

A MINING TOWN GENERAL STORE

STAND AND DELIVER!

Traveling through the West could be dangerous for many reasons. For one, gangs of highwaymen often preyed on travelers. These were thieves who stopped stagecoaches at gunpoint and robbed the people on board.

The miners themselves could be a rowdy bunch. In 1861, Central City recorded 217 fistfights, 97 revolver fights, 11 Bowie knife fights, and one dogfight.

A SALOON IN AN OLD WESTERN TOWN

Everyone was there for the same reason—to make money.

Most people tried to do so honestly, but not everyone. Pickpockets, thieves, and cheaters were naturally attracted to such a scene. Here were lots of people, lots of money, and no real police!

Grifters, or con artists—people who trick innocent folks out of their money—were mixed in with the crowds. Typically, such tricksters are good actors. They begin by winning people's trust through charm and friendliness.

NOT SO CLEAN

"Soapy" Smith (1860–1898) was Colorado's most notorious con artist and gangster. He operated in Creede and Denver.

Men gamble in a saloon in Telluride while, at the right, the sheriff leans against the bar.

Once they hoodwink, or fool, their victim, the fake friend quickly disappears and moves on to the next town or camp.

Communities were naturally eager to establish law and order. Towns elected a sheriff to be the head law enforcement agent, with deputies, or assistants, to help him. Throughout the American frontier, sheriffs helped to tame the "Wild" West.

KNOWLEDGE NUGGET

Bat Masterson (1853–1921) was a famous lawman and gambler in Kansas and Colorado.

A COWBOY OF THE OLD WEST

HANDS UP!

David J. Cook, a Colorado sheriff in the 1860s, wrote a book of advice for law enforcement agents in the West. His 1882 book was called *Hands Up! or Twenty Years of Detective Life in the Mountains and on the Plains.*

A sample of his advice: "Never hit a prisoner over the head with your pistol, because you may afterwards want to use your weapon and find it disabled."

CHAPTER 11

Boomtowns and Ghost Towns

Mining camps often grew into towns. Some of them, such as Central City, Leadville, and Cripple Creek, became **boomtowns**. The gold rush (and 20 years later, the silver boom) produced many such places in Colorado. Aspen, Crested Butte, Breckenridge, and Telluride all began as gold-mining boomtowns.

In August 1859, a newspaper reported, "Although not three months old, [Mountain City] contains already some 300 buildings substantially erected, with a population of between 2,800 and 3,000, nearly all of whom

The region's first post office opened in Denver. It served as the address of thousands of gold rushers, who received about 12,500 letters per week.

The Central City/Black Hawk Historic District, once called the "Richest Square Mile on Earth" is now an official National Historic Landmark.

are miners. Yet the arts and trades are well represented, we have about 25 stores, 2 jewelry shops, 3 tailor shops, blacksmiths, shoemakers, painters, etc." Mountain City soon became the boomtown Central City.

Denver began life in 1858. Most gold seekers first arrived in Denver and would set out from there, so the town quickly became a supply hub. Boomtowns like Denver offered shops, livestock trading, gambling, and saloons for the miners' entertainment.

Saloons were more than just places to get a drink. Miners could relax, discuss news, and play cards, billiards, and darts. Some saloons featured dancing girls, piano players, and even theatrical skits. Before long, theaters and music halls appeared.

In June 1860, the Western Stage Company began running daily stagecoaches from Denver to Mountain City. The 35-mile (56 km) ride took seven to eight hours. A year earlier, it had taken three or four days. Today it takes about 47 minutes.

DENVER IN 1898

The silver-mining boomtown of Bonanza City, for example, once had two hotels, 16 dance halls, 26 saloons, a newspaper, grocery and clothing stores, a candy store, and even a town baseball team.

An old gold mine in Cripple Creek But if you are not familiar with it, that could be because the town barely exists today. In 2014, Bonanza, Colorado, had a population of one.

Oro City, near Leadville, was once home to 10,000 people. Today it has a population of zero. Once the mining dried up, some boomtowns became **ghost towns**. Without the mines, there was no reason for people to remain, and they simply all moved away. In some cases, the towns were not completely abandoned. However, so many people and businesses left that the towns became mere shadows of their former glory days.

Some towns, such as Central City, were able to adapt and become tourist centers. Some

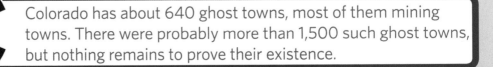

Colorado has about 640 ghost towns, most of them mining towns. There were probably more than 1,500 such ghost towns, but nothing remains to prove their existence.

According to
the Colorado Division of
Reclamation, Mining, and Safety,
there are more than 23,000
abandoned mines in
Colorado.

St. Elmo is a ghost town that tourists can visit.

ghost towns, such as St. Elmo in Chaffee
County, have been preserved and function
like museums.

Mining was not always the cause of ghostly
towns. Some of Colorado's phantoms are old
farming towns on the Eastern Plains. In some
cases, rural towns were deserted as people
moved to the cities. Others were resort towns
that never brought in enough tourists.

One of
Colorado's most famous
ghost towns is Buckskin Joe, once
the county seat of Park County. It was a
gold-mining town named for one of the
prospectors, who wore buckskin
clothing.

39

CHAPTER 12

The Denver Mint

A mint is an herb, and a mint is a candy with a refreshing flavor. A mint is also a place that manufactures coins out of metals. The Denver Mint is the type that makes coins, not candy.

At the beginning of the gold rush, the office of Clark, Gruber & Company opened in Denver. This company made coins out of the miners' gold dust and nuggets. The first coin was an 1860 $10 gold piece. It pictured Pikes Peak on its face with the words Pikes Peak Gold encircling the summit. On its back was an American eagle. Eventually the company created $2.50, $5, and $20 coins as well. These coins were for private collectors. They were not official U.S. money.

In 1863, the U.S. government bought the company and opened the U.S. **Assay** Office in its place. This office melted down the miners' gold and cast it into gold bars stamped with the metal's weight and quality.

U.S. coins are no longer made out of silver or gold. Those metals are simply too valuable to use in regular money!

LOADING COINS AT THE DENVER MINT

EVERY COIN HAS A BIRTHMARK

Mint marks show which minting facility a coin came from. "D" is for Denver, "P" is for Philadelphia, and "S" for San Francisco. The tiny letter can be found to the right of the subject's face on the coin. Denver's "D" used to stand for "Dahlonega" (Georgia), a branch of the U.S. Mint that closed during the Civil War.

In 1904, the U.S. government built a grand new building in Denver. It converted the assay office into a new branch of the U.S. Mint to make official U.S. coins. Today, the Denver Mint can produce more than 50 million coins a day.

Citizens of Denver took refuge in the old Denver Mint building in 1864 when they heard rumors of possible Indian attacks.

CHAPTER 13

Colorado Territory

The Colorado Territory ceased to exist in 1876, when statehood was finally granted to Colorado.

The discovery of gold in the Rocky Mountains transformed the course of history. By 1859, changes were happening with astonishing speed! The huge influx of gold seekers brought the first significant population of nonnative people to the region.

In the years before the gold rush, Colorado was divided among four official U.S. territories—the Kansas, Utah, Nebraska, and New Mexico territories. On February 28, 1861, the U.S. Congress created a new territory, the Colorado Territory. Its borders were identical with those of the state today.

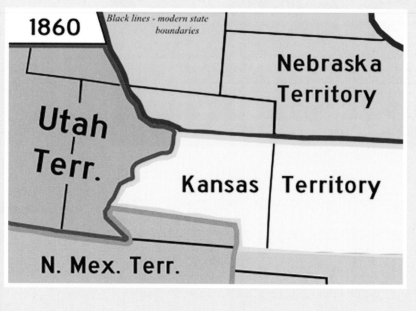

1860   Black lines - modern state boundaries

Nebraska Territory

Utah Terr.

Kansas | Territory

N. Mex. Terr.

Much of this land had been under Indian control. The Ute and Shoshone people controlled much of the western part of the new territory. The Eastern Plains were more loosely held by a mix of Cheyenne, Arapaho, and other Plains tribes. Just ten days before the establishment of the Colorado Territory, the U.S. government compelled the Indians to give up claims to this land.

The new residents of the Colorado Territory immediately began asking for statehood. In fact, Colorado probably would have become a state sooner than it did, but there was a major complicating factor.

In 1861, the country was in the midst of the American Civil War. Potential statehood was complicated by questions of whether the new state would side with the Confederacy (the Southern states that had broken away from the United States) and permit slavery. As a territory, however, the region could be kept under Union control.

KNOWLEDGE NUGGET

In 1863, the town of Golden became the capital of the new territory. The people of Denver were disappointed. But they wouldn't be disappointed for long. Denver City became the capital in 1869.

CHAPTER 14

Most Bust, Some Boom

In the end, the Pikes Peak gold rush was both a bust and a boom. It changed lives, and it changed history. It certainly changed the United States.

Most fortune hunters were disappointed. Most had rushed to Colorado with unrealistic expectations. They were bedazzled by rumors and misleading newspaper reports. Folks who expected to get rich quick the easy way were the first ones to give up. Bust!

However, many stayed and worked hard. For some of them, there really was gold at the end of the rainbow.

By the mid-1860s, however, the gold boom was already beginning to wane. Miners dug out all the shallow gold veins they could find. Their equipment simply couldn't get at the stuff buried in deeper ores. Many miners stayed in Colorado and became farmers, ranchers,

In 1887, America's largest gold nugget was discovered in Breckenridge, Colorado. It weighed 13 pounds, 7 ounces.

A bright rainbow shines over Grand Junction, Colorado.

merchants, and politicians. They built new
communities and raised families. They also
developed new industries. Within decades,
for example, new techniques were developed
for getting at the deeper **ores**. Gold and silver
mining became major Colorado industries.

For the country, the gold rush was a boom.
It led to the formation of a great state. The Fifty-
Niners had gone searching for gold, but they
found something even better. Colorado!

The purity of gold is measured in karats.
Pure gold equals 24 karats (K).Gold nuggets
range from approximately 92 percent to 99.6
percent pure gold—approximately 22 K to 24 K

Glossary

assay—the testing of metal or ore to determine its quality

boomtown—a town that grows rapidly due to sudden prosperity

bullion—pure gold (or silver) in bulk form, usually in bars or bricks, bearing a stamped weight

ghost town—a once-flourishing town with few or no remaining inhabitants

gold rush—a rapid influx of people looking to find gold

gulch—a narrow, steep-sided ravine, usually with a rushing stream at the bottom

hit pay dirt—pay dirt is soil or ore that has gold or other valuable mineral in it. The phrase has come to mean "find what you are looking for" or "get rich."

intrinsic value—built-in goodness; the essential worth that something has just by its very nature

lode—a vein of metal ore in the earth

metal—a solid material that is typically hard and shiny, which can be worked into different shapes without breaking or cracking. Gold, silver, copper, iron, and aluminum are metals.

metallurgy—the science and technology of metals.

nugget—a small lump of gold found in the earth

ore—a mineral or rock that contains metal

panning for gold—a method of finding gold dust in a stream

placer gold—gold that has weathered out from its source

prospectors—people who look for mineral deposits, usually gold, in the ground

stake a claim—to mark out the parcel of land where one is prospecting. Today, the phrase has come to mean "declare one's right to, or ownership of, something."

streambed—the dirt bottom of a stream or creek

strike it rich—to strike a vein of gold. Today it means to "become wealthy suddenly or unexpectedly."

veins—in geology, a vein is a distinct streak of a certain mineral, such as gold, that runs through a rock

Index

Due to the changing nature of Internet links, the Rosen Publishing Group, Inc., has developed an online list of websites related to the subject of this book. This site is updated regularly. Please use this link to access the list:
http://www.powerkidslinks.com/soco/ppgr